ACCELERATE

A FRAMEWORK FOR **BUSINESS OWNERS**
TO CREATE LASTING **SUCCESS**

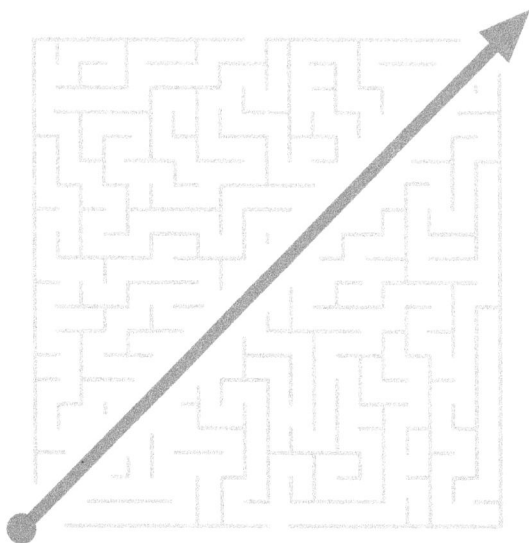

ACCELERATE

CHRIS GREEN

Published in 2025 by Chris Green
chris@chrisgreen.au
www.chrisgreen.au

Cover design: Tess McCabe
Editor: Andrew Campbell

ISBN: 9781923403925 (pbk)
ISBN: 9781923403932 (ebk)

A catalogue record for this book is available from the National Library of Australia.

Contents

About the Author

Chris Green works with entrepreneurs across Australia and New Zealand to help them break through what's holding them back and build businesses that work for them, not the other way around. Over 25 years, he's worked with hundreds of business owners who felt stuck despite running successful businesses on paper. People describe Chris as approachable – the kind of person you'd chat with at the barbecue, who believes you can be serious about business without taking yourself too seriously. His focus is helping business owners find clarity, capability, and confidence using a proven Success System. Chris is the creator of the Accelerate program and the Business by Design mentoring program. He is host of The Green Room podcast, and he keeps things grounded, practical, and real.

Introduction

Business By Design, Not Default

You didn't start your business to burn out. You started it with energy, with a vision, and a belief that you could do something better, and do it differently. But somewhere along the way, that clarity got buried under a pile of half-finished tasks, endless decisions, and the constant feeling that if *you* stop, *everything* stops.

If that sounds familiar, you're not alone. I've worked with hundreds of business owners who hit what I call the 'entrepreneurial ceiling' – that invisible threshold where your growth stalls, not because you lack skill or drive, but because your bandwidth is maxed out. You're doing good work, but it's reactive, not strategic. You're putting out fires instead of building something scalable. The business runs on your energy, and the moment you take a breath, it all starts to wobble.

This book is about how you can do things differently.

My in-person Accelerate business program (and what you'll find in this text version) has been built on what I've learned from mentoring business owners for 25 years, and from running my own businesses. It is a step-by-step framework to help you build a business that works. It will help you create practices and processes that are consistent, scalable, values-driven, and profitable. Accelerate is the distillation of decades of work with startups, growing companies, and ambitious founders who are ready to break through the entrepreneurial ceiling and create something that is sustainable and impactful.

In the eight-week Accelerate learning program, I teach the 'Success System', which empowers business owners to dig deep on eight fundamental elements of business success:

1. **Your legacy** – Defining the impact and ripple effect that you want your business to create in the world.

2. **Your values, behaviour and reputation** – Aligning who you are with how your business shows up every day.

3. **Your horizon** – Creating a clear long-term vision that pulls you forward.

4. **Your implementation cadence** – Translating your vision into a practical execution system.

5. **Your product** – Building a monopoly through focus, differentiation, and quality.

6. **Your people** – Developing a team who believe in your mission and who can and will amplify your success.

7. **Your promotion** – Communicating your value in a way that resonates and converts into sales and customer/client engagement.

8. **Your profit** – Using financial insight to fund your growth, freedom, and future.

Figure 1: The Success System

As shown in the model, the heart of sustainable business growth is the combination of your Eco System, Business System, and Operating System. The **Eco System** represents your values, legacy, and reputation, which are the deeper *why* behind your business. The **Business System** maps your strategic vision, from your 10-year horizon down to 90-day campaigns, providing a clear sense of *possibility*. And the **Operating System** is where strategy meets day-to-day action – your people, product, and promotion – which drives real-world *execution*. These three systems are held together by the crucial glue of *alignment*, ensuring every part of your business moves in sync, not in silos. When possibility, alignment, and execution are all working together, you create a business that's not only successful, but is also sustainable, energising, and impactful.

And underpinning all of this work is a core belief: that you don't need to build a business by default. You get to choose, you get to design, you get to lead. This isn't a book of quick hacks and short-term solutions. It's a roadmap for thoughtful business owners like you who are ready to move from reactive to proactive, from tired to empowered, and from chaotic to consistent.

Wherever you're starting from, you're not behind. You're exactly where you need to be to begin building your business by design.

CHAPTER 1

THE ENTREPRENEURIAL CEILING AND THE POWER OF DESIGN

I f you're like most small business owners, you didn't start your business to feel overwhelmed, or to struggle through your week. You started it because you had a vision, a skill, a product, or a service you believed could make a difference to your clients/customers, and to the world. Maybe you wanted more freedom, more impact, or simply to do work your way. But somewhere along the way, the thing you built began to trap you.

I've been there – when I owned and ran a pub in regional Victoria in my twenties – and so have hundreds of the founders and owners I've worked with. There's this moment when your business stops feeling exciting and starts feeling exhausting. You get to the point where you're maxed out. You can't delegate. You say yes to too much. And no matter how hard you work, it feels like you're falling further behind.

The ceiling you didn't know you were building

In the early stages of business – startup, high growth, and capacity – you wear every hat (see Figure 2). You sell, you deliver, you invoice, you solve, you do all the admin, and you clean up. In the startup phase, it's exciting but messy. In high growth, the leads start flowing and things feel like they're working. Then you hit capacity and the cracks start to show. You become defined by your energy; or lack thereof.

You might think, 'I only work 17 hours a day, 7 days a week, and rest of the time is mine'. But this tongue-in-cheek thinking sees you resentful of the world you've created.

	LIFECYCLE	FOCUS	STATE
BREAKTHROUGH	Scalable	Visionary	Rewarding
	Consistent	Systems-driven	Sustainable
	Transitional	Leveraged	Developmental
BUILD UP	Capacity	Chaotic	Overwhelm
	High growth	Customer-driven	Reactive
	Startup	Creative	Uncommercial

Figure 2: The Business by Design Value Model

When you're in the capacity stage, you're producing more than ever before. You've got more customers, but you're also exhausted. Your systems are half-baked or non-existent. You're making it work through sheer force of will. But that's when the entrepreneurial ceiling appears.

The entrepreneurial ceiling forms when you, the founder, become the limit of your own business. Everything in the business (and in fact the success of the business) depends on you – your energy, your availability, your decision-making. But when you hit your limit, everything starts slipping: your delivery/product, the client experience, staff engagement, and especially your joy.

The business stops working for you; and you start working for the business. That was never the dream. You want to get through to the point of breakthrough, but you just don't know how you can work any more or any harder.

Tinkering won't break the ceiling

When they sense things aren't quite right, most business owners try to fix the symptoms – they tinker, they hire more people, they try a new CRM… Maybe they bring on a coach to 'get organised'. But none of that works – at least not long-term – unless they address the fundamental organisational structure.

To break through the entrepreneurial ceiling, you need more than a better to-do list; you need a better game plan.

That's what my Success System (the process) and Success Map (the tool) are designed to do. As you're reading this book, I invite you to reimagine your business from the inside out, not by focusing on what you should do, but by exploring what you could do. The real breakthrough comes when you stop trying to do everything yourself and start building a business that can thrive without your constant involvement. That transformation begins with one key step: the transition phase.

Transition is not a tweak – it's a transformation

The transition to get through the entrepreneurial ceiling and out of chaos into clarity doesn't happen overnight, yet this is the part most people underestimate. On average, it takes two years to get above the line, where you leverage what's in your head into a repeatable, systems-driven, robust business model. The time it takes will be frustrating, unpredictable, and at times will make you feel like you're moving backwards... But as Robin Sharma says, this is the messy middle that you need to work through.

It will be a slow process. You might delegate something, and it won't go well. You'll document a process and then discover it's not scalable. You'll take your hands off something... and be tempted to snatch it back when it doesn't go perfectly. As Brene Brown says, this is the point where we need to lean into the discomfort; because this is where the real transformation happens.

In breaking through the entrepreneurial ceiling, you build systems, processes, and people that support your business growth. Eventually, these systems, processes, and people help you design a business that is leveraged, consistent, and scalable. Your business will thrive because of the systems you've created, and because it no longer solely relies on you.

The Success System: A map for change

To guide this journey, I developed a framework called the **Success System**. It divides your transformation into five actionable phases:

1. **Commit** – Decide that things need to change and shift your mindset.
2. **Foundation** – Build cultural and operational readiness.

3. **Direction** – Set clear, inspiring goals and long-term plans.

4. **Execution** – Align your daily actions with your strategic vision.

5. **Design** – Intentionally create the business you've always wanted.

This framework isn't theoretical; it encourages you to get out of your head and into the practicalities. It's designed to help you move away from firefighting and towards focus. However, it only works if you commit to it – fully.

Throughout this book, we'll unpack the elements of the Success System.

Three systems, one business

Within the Success System I consider your business to be not just one thing; rather, it is made up of three key elements:

1. The **Eco System**: This is your purpose, your values, and your legacy. The Eco System answers the question: *Who are we? And what do we want our broader contribution to be?*

2. The **Business System**: This is your vision and strategy. The Business System answers: *Where are we going and how will we get there?*

3. The **Operating System**: This is your execution engine. The Operating System answers: *What do we do every day to deliver consistently and grow?*

Throughout this book, I move through these three systems in order and unpack the 12 pillars that make up the full Success System. Let's first focus on the Eco System, which is the part that most business leave out, as they skip straight to the doing and/or the product. The Eco System is the absolute foundation that all great businesses are built from.

The first key driver of the Eco System is the one that we get out of bed for, the one that lights us up, and the one that builds the scaffolding to stay the course: legacy.

Legacy: The ripples you leave

Legacy isn't just about the end of your life and what you leave behind. It's about the impact you make now that will ripple outward into the future. I often use a metaphor to explain the idea of legacy: imagine throwing a rock into a still pond. You see the splash. But what continues to resonate are the ripples that follow. You can't control exactly where they go or what they look like, but you can control the size of the rock and the intention and direction behind the throw.

Your legacy is the ripple.

I define legacy using three core ideas:

1. **Personal fulfilment** – Does your impact light you up?
2. **Inspiration for others** – Are you leading in a way that uplifts and motivates?
3. **Perpetuating values** – Are you building something that outlasts you?

If your legacy is just about status, success, or money, it won't stick, it won't be enduring, and it won't stand the test of time. But if it's rooted in genuine purpose and contribution, it becomes your anchor – especially during challenging times.

Brushstroke by brushstroke

One of my favourite stories is that of Van Gogh, Picasso and da Vinci – all of whom painted multiple masterpieces on repurposed canvases. Beneath many of their famous works, there's an earlier painting that they weren't satisfied with. They didn't start from scratch each time on a new canvas; instead, they painted over what was there, brushstroke by brushstroke, and created something that was priceless and timeless.

That's how I want you to think about your business – like a canvas you're painting over. You're not throwing it out, you're rebuilding – intentionally – on the canvas you already have. This isn't about overnight success; rather, it's about deliberate design, and it's about painting over your canvas, brush stroke by brush stroke, until your new painting appears.

Before we move on, here's the challenge. Stop and ask yourself: are you building a business that reflects what truly matters to you, or one that just keeps you busy? Defining your legacy isn't a box to tick; it should be the cornerstone of everything that follows.

In the next chapter, we'll bring that legacy to life by embedding your values into the fabric of your business. Because culture doesn't happen by accident – it's built, intentionally, from the inside out.

CHAPTER 2

DEFINING WHAT MATTERS

WHAT DO YOU WANT TO BE KNOWN FOR?

When I ask business owners what they want to be known for, I often get silence. Not because they lack ambition or vision, but often because no one's asked them that before. What I have learned about business owners is that they can get swept up in the momentum of building. They're chasing leads, hiring staff, fixing problems, hitting targets. But somewhere in the blur of activity, the business starts to shape them and their life too much, rather than the other way around.

This chapter is about reclaiming that direction. It's about building a business that reflects who you are, what you believe in, and how you want to show up in the world.

Before you plan, and before you execute, you need to decide who you are. That's the essence of the Eco System. It's not about products, processes, or profits; it's about your identity, integrity, and intention. Without clarity around your identity, integrity, and intention, your decision-making is erratic, your culture is reactive, and your reputation is inconsistent. But with a strong foundation, you move from reactivity to where you're in control, and you have belief in your future direction.

In this chapter we explore three powerful concepts that round out the Eco System: your values, your behaviours, and your reputation. These are the tools that shape your business from the inside out and define your identity, integrity, and intention within your business and with your clients/customers.

Defining your values: The beliefs that guide the work

Let's start with values. Values aren't just what you write on the wall; they're not the posters in your boardroom or the buzzwords in your 'About Us' page on your website. Values are your *true north*, and they are especially important when the pressure is on.

I consider business values in three dimensions:

1. **Beliefs** – These are what you stand for. They are non-negotiable principles that inform every decision.
2. **Attitudes** – The energy and positioning that your business brings to the world – how you respond, how you lead, how you show up.
3. **Behaviours** – These are the real test. They are the things you do consistently, especially when no one is watching.

Your values aren't real until they show up in your behaviours, and that's why I tell owners and leaders: *Whether you like it or not, you are constantly communicating your values.* For example, if you say you value collaboration but you tolerate passive-aggressive behaviour in team meetings, what value is being reinforced? It isn't collaboration. If you say you stand for quality, but you rush delivery without proper quality assurance, you've just undermined your own foundation. Consistency between your beliefs and behaviours is what creates your identity.

The journey of the apprentice: A lesson in culture by contradiction

I've heard this story so many times I've lost count. Once upon a time, a young, baby-faced sparkie – an apprentice electrician – eager and wide-eyed, steps into the world of his chosen trade. On his very first day, he's welcomed with ceremony and purpose. The electrical organisation runs a high-powered induction designed to set the tone: *This is who we are. We show up on time. We work hard. We live our values. We earn our rewards.*

The message is clear, bold, and inspiring – a call to excellence. The apprentice feels the weight of that invitation. He's ready to rise to it.

But the next day, the real test begins, not in a classroom but on the job site.

He's paired with one of the organisation's longest-serving tradies, a seasoned figure in this world – his guide, his mentor. At 7 am sharp, they get to work. The apprentice watches carefully, mimicking every move, eager to prove himself. He remembers the words from the day before and holds them close.

Then it's morning tea. They head to the local café, part of an unspoken tradition. The mentor orders his usual: a coffee and a meat pie. The apprentice follows suit. They sit. They chat. Laughter flows. Time passes. The 15-minute break, outlined in yesterday's induction, stretches into 25 minutes.

The apprentice looks around. No rush. No accountability. No urgency.

And in that moment, the real lesson is learned, not from a slideshow, but from lived behaviour. Here lies the contradiction: the culture he was *told* versus the culture he was *shown*.

So, what sticks?

The apprentice has a choice. He can believe what was said… or follow what is done. And most do the latter. This is the quiet crossroads where culture is forged, not in the words we speak, but in the habits we tolerate and the behaviours we model.

Practise what you preach

If you lead a team, your behaviours aren't just observed by your colleagues and employees, they're absorbed. Culture is not a memo; it's a mirror – and that mirror reflects everything you *do* and everything you *let slide*. When I owned my restaurant, it was defined not only by what meals I served, but by what I *didn't* serve.

There's a model I often share, which I adapted from Meredith Wilson's book *Shift: Everyday Actions Leaders Can Take to Shift Culture*. This simplifies leadership into two phrases:

1. What we demonstrate.
2. What we tolerate.

You demonstrate values through your own choices. But you also shape the culture through what you allow to happen unaddressed. That's the second layer of leadership that many people miss. It's similar to how the success of great movies can be attributed to what is left on the cutting room floor as much as what makes the final edit.

Let me be clear: nothing erodes culture faster than inconsistent leadership and misalignment between what we demonstrate and what we tolerate. A single instance of disrespect, laziness, or manipulation left unchecked will ripple through a team.

Inconsistent leadership drives inconsistent outcomes. This inconsistency is observed, heard, witnessed, and noted by everyone you lead.

As a leader, you set the standard, not just in what you do, but in what you hold others accountable for. That is how we multiply the culture we want. We engage in behaviours that define the culture we want, rather than engaging in behaviours that defy the culture we want.

You might have heard the saying 'A fish rots from the head down'. When it comes to culture, and a leader's role in creating the desired culture, this statement is fitting. If you can't walk the walk, you shouldn't talk the talk.

Moments of truth: What your clients see

While your team experiences your internal values and behaviours, your clients/customers encounter them externally – often without you realising it. This happens in the critical interactions between a customer and a business that Jan Carlzon (1987) calls 'moments of truth'. Moments of truth are the small, seemingly inconsequential touchpoints that make or break trust with our clients/customers, including:

· An invoice paid late.
· A poorly worded email.
· A broken link on your website.
· A staff member who sounds uninterested on a phone call.
· An inquiry that goes unanswered.

In isolation, these moments might seem minor to you. However, taken together, they form a picture. They tell your customers who you are, and – whether you like it or not – your reputation is built (or broken) in these micro-moments.

Think about when you fill your car up at the petrol station. You step out of your car into a puddle, the pump handle is covered in grease, the assistants are deep in conversation when you go to pay for your fuel and barely acknowledge you... These are the moments of truth that send a clear message that defines your customer journey and reflects where your business is at.

At this point I challenge you to walk through your customer journey – from enquiry to delivery to follow-up – and ask: *What are we really demonstrating? What do they see when they engage with us? Is this aligned with what we say we care about ourselves and how we want to treat our customers?*

Reputation: What you're (currently) known for

If legacy is what you want to be remembered for, then reputation is what you're known for now. It's the sum of your values, behaviours, and moments of truth – reflected back to you by the marketplace. But here's the kicker: you don't get to decide your reputation. The market does.

However, you *do* get to shape it.

Every business builds a reputation, not just by what they say, but by how they behave when the customer isn't watching. The businesses with the best reputations earn their name by consistently doing four things well: delivering **operational excellence**, being **highly responsive**, communicating **clearly and consistently**, and most importantly, **exceeding expectations**. When you can execute all four of these things consistently, your customers don't just trust you; they rely on you, advocate for you, and keep coming back.

Case study: Leading the conversation

An engineering design firm I worked with knew their craft inside and out. Technically speaking, they were experts: brilliant designers, deep thinkers, and very sharp with details. But in the eyes of the customer, something wasn't landing. Their work was solid, but their responsiveness was slow. Communication lacked clarity. Customers often had to chase them for updates. They were 'safe', the kind of business you could trust to get the job done – eventually – but they weren't standout. In short, they were caught up in the day to day. They were busy being busy to the point where they lived in the technical dimension and forgot about the customer.

I worked with the team to change customer perceptions. They started responding faster, explaining things in plain language, and actively managing client expectations. They began spotting issues before they escalated, offering design solutions that weren't just accurate but also made the projects smoother for the fabricator.

That's when the shift happened in client perceptions. They moved beyond just knowing the answer to **leading the conversation**. Clients no longer just respected and relied on their drawings; they respected *how* they showed up. That's the difference between being an expert and becoming an industry leader. And occasionally, when timeframes were tight, they went above and beyond to save a project in trouble – not because they had to, but because they could. That's what great businesses do. They don't just say it, they live it – every conversation, every deadline, every drawing – it all adds up to reputation.

You shape your reputation by delivering on your promises, by consistently aligning your actions with your stated values, and by deliberately crafting the stories, testimonials, and evidence that validate your brand. Your business reputation is a fragile and powerful resource; it allows you to launch new products or services, and borrow capital. But when your reputation is damaged, rebuilding it is slow and uncertain. That's why I encourage you to protect it like it's your most valuable asset – because it is. It is the hardest resource to obtain; and it is the easiest to lose.

The reputation flywheel

The best way to build your reputation is to move the flywheel. This concept, from Jim Collins' book *Good to Great: Why Some Companies Make the Leap... And Others Don't*, is simple but profound. You build momentum through consistent, aligned action. One good customer experience doesn't make you legendary, but it starts the flywheel moving – albeit slowly. Over time, with more and more positive experiences, reviews, and testimonials, the flywheel starts moving by itself, and it becomes faster and faster as you build momentum.

There are four ways to get the flywheel moving:

1. **Process and systems** – Building internal consistency and quality assurance.
2. **Track record** – Building a history of results.
3. **Market visibility** – Being seen by a qualified prospect/ potential client.
4. **Market alignment** – Being valued by the market for your product or service.

Process and systems

Momentum isn't accidental – it's engineered through intentional, repeatable processes. When a business invests in systems that ensure consistency and quality, it creates a reliable experience for every customer, not just a lucky few. This infrastructure becomes the backbone of excellence for your business, by removing guesswork and freeing up mental bandwidth for growth. It's the discipline behind the scenes that quietly powers long-term success, as it leverages the knowledge of the key people in the organisation and translates it into everyday practice for all employees.

Track record

Your credibility compounds. Every time you deliver on a promise, meet a deadline, or exceed expectations, you contribute to a growing track record with your customers that builds trust. Over time, this consistent performance becomes a key part of your reputation, which becomes something that precedes you in the market and reassures prospective clients. A strong track record provides evidence to the market that you can solve their problems, meet their demands, and service their needs.

Market visibility

You can be the best-kept secret, or you can be seen. But visibility, when strategic, is not about shouting louder – it's about showing up in the right places, to the right people, to those who need your product or service, and are able to buy. At the end of the day, you can't sell a secret. In a service business, qualified prospects need to know, like, and trust you. But if they can't see you, they can't build connection and therefore can't build trust. On the other hand, when qualified prospects see your value on display, you become a familiar, trusted option.

Market alignment

Even the best offer falls flat if the market doesn't need or want what you are selling. Market alignment is about ensuring that your product or service addresses real needs, resonates with current desires, and delivers value in the eyes of your ideal customer. It's where relevance meets demand, and like the tractor beam in *Star Wars*, which pulls the Millenium Falcon towards the Death Star, it creates a natural pull towards you rather than a push. When your business solves meaningful problems, the momentum builds itself, and there will be more inward traffic than outbound marketing.

The main message here is that reputation, ultimately, isn't just a lever in your business – it's actually the engine room of growth and scalability. While some research highlights reputation as one of many growth factors in business, I believe it to be *the one* that has the greatest impact. Without a strong and growing reputation, businesses remain founder-reliant, unable to scale beyond individual capability and knowledge. But with it, information is transferred, opportunities multiply, and the business earns the right to grow at speed – beyond the founder, beyond the noise, and into something enduring.

Over time, this consistent motion in all four areas builds a self-reinforcing engine of trust and demand. But like any flywheel, it takes *effort* to get moving. If you don't apply consistent effort to maintain momentum, the flywheel will inevitably grind to a halt. But if you continue to lean on the flywheel and invest consistent effort, the weight of your effort will begin to turn the flywheel for you. When that happens, clients come to you, talent wants to work for you, and opportunities find you. That's the compound effect of a reputation built by design. The flywheel builds its own momentum, ultimately gathers speed, and drives business growth.

In the next chapter, we'll move from solid foundations to planning your future. We'll look at how to shape your direction, how to dream bigger, plan smarter, and lead with purpose. But for now, focus on the business you're becoming. That's the business the world will experience; and eventually, it will be the business they remember.

CHAPTER 3

THINK BIGGER

BUILDING A FUTURE WORTH LEADING TOWARDS

I f the first two chapters of this journey were about reminding yourself who you are and what your business stands for, this one is about who you are becoming – and what your business is capable of. This is the chapter where we stop tinkering at the edges of today's business and start designing the business of the future. It's where we begin to think bigger.

I know that phrase gets thrown around a lot, but in my world, 'thinking bigger' isn't something that's just written on a motivational poster – it's a disciplined, strategic stretch. It means opening up the space between what's probable and what's possible and giving yourself the permission, and the process, to explore that space fully.

The horizon is the point, not the place

When I ask business owners to look 10 years ahead, most of them squint. Not because they lack ambition, but because they've never really been asked to dream that far ahead in concrete, strategic terms. They've been in the thick of today's problems for so long – cash flow, hiring, product tweaks, delivery challenges – that looking out to the horizon feels… distant. Abstract. Maybe even a little self-indulgent.

But let me tell you this: **The 10-year horizon is a magnificent way of ideating what's possible**.

The 10-year horizon is not a prediction; rather, it's a direction that gives all your short-term decisions meaning. When talking about the 10-year horizon, I always think of the Bill Gates quote: 'Most people overestimate what they can do in one year and underestimate what they can do in 10.' I've seen this play out again and again with business owners. Owners who set big, audacious 10-year goals – even if they fall short – end up building something far greater than those who only think in the short-term.

And that's the point. A 10-year horizon won't give you certainty, but it will give you clarity.

Probable. Preferable. Possible.

When you think about the future, I want you to hold the three futures from futurist Professor Jim Dator in your mind:

1. **The probable future** – This is business-as-usual and the logical extension of your current trajectory. You keep doing what you're doing, maybe with some tweaks, while playing it safe. There's comfort in the prospect of the probable future, but it's actually the most unlikely of futures – because the only certainty we have is change.

2. **The preferable future** – This is the version of your business you *want* to build, as it's where your current plans and strategies are aimed. It's achievable, but it requires changes: better systems, higher capacity in your people, more focused effort, and a clearer strategy.

The preferable future should have an element of truth and resonance to it, because this is what we can imagine is possible.

3. **The possible future** – This is the future that's not limited by current constraints, because it's the big stretch. It asks: *What could happen if you stopped playing small?* Or: *What if your business solved a much bigger problem than it does today?* Or even: *What if you scaled in a way you hadn't dared to imagine?* Every successful visionary leader I've worked with has taken the risk of playing in the possible future space. They've played well beyond their current-day constraints and dreamed bigger than they ever thought possible.

Futurists like Sohail Inayatullah, Otto Scharmer, and Alex Hagan talk about the difference between 'seeing' and 'being'. When you think about the future, it's not just about forecasting trends; it's about becoming the kind of business that can meet and shape those trends.

Being in service

I love asking clients the question: *What's the biggest problem your business could solve in 10 years' time?* I'm not talking about adding a few clients or doubling your revenue. I'm talking about the kind of challenge that, if your business took it on, would transform your market, or even the world. Like the idea of your possible future, or the concept of '10× your business' by Dan Sullivan and Dr Benjamin Hardy, this is your **moonshot**. And no, it doesn't need to be polished or perfectly feasible. It just needs to be ambitious.

It needs to be ambitious because ambition pulls you forward to seek new horizons; it makes today's chaos worth navigating, it gives your team something to believe in, and it gets you exploring the gap between what is now and what could be in 10 years' time. As a result, we consider how to build capacity in our people, enter new markets, develop new products and services, and increase equity. And when you name it, and start building towards it, something powerful happens: *you start seeing opportunities you never saw before.*

From vision to strategy: The hedgehog concept

I love the notion of the hedgehog concept, as proposed by Jim Collins in his book *Good to Great: Why Some Companies Make the Leap... And Others Don't.* When faced with danger, a hedgehog doesn't try a dozen clever manoeuvres – it curls into a ball and uses its quills. It uses one strategy. One big thing.

The best businesses do the same; they don't chase every shiny idea. They build around *one big idea* – which is a clear and compelling vision that guides everything from product to hiring to marketing. Jim Collins and Jerry Porras refer to this idea as a 'big hairy audacious goal' (or BHAG) in their book *Built to Last: Successful Habits of Visionary Companies*; and Chris McChesney, Sean Covey, and Jim Huling refer to this as a 'wildly important goal' (WIG) in *The 4 Disciplines of Execution*.

Your job as a leader is to figure out what that one big thing is for your business and then learn how to communicate it with clarity. Think of it like your vision pitch: If I sat next to you on a plane and asked where your business will be in 10 years' time, could you answer me in 90 seconds or less? If not, keep refining your thinking until you can.

The power of mission

When everyone on your team knows the mission, decision-making becomes faster, easier, and more aligned. That's one of the lessons from *Extreme Ownership*, a brilliant book by Jocko Willink and Leif Babin. When they led Navy SEAL teams in combat zones, they learned that *clarity of mission* was everything. It wasn't just about orders; it was about alignment. Everyone needed to understand the objective and believe in it.

Now, you are obviously not leading troops into battle, but you are leading people through uncertainty, change, and growth. And if your team only sees a to-do list rather than genuinely understanding the mission, they'll never truly know the significance of their role in the broader vision.

That's why we start with the 10-year horizon – we build the mission from the top down. Because a clearly defined purpose doesn't just inspire – it guides people out of the weeds, and the day-to-day operational demands that occupy their thinking, into bigger and broader strategic decision-making.

From 10-year horizon to three-year goal

Once your big, ambitious vision is defined, the next step is setting a tangible three-year goal. This isn't about evenly splitting the numbers or aspirations into thirds in a tokenistic plan. It's about strategically asking: *What must we do in the next three years to be on track for the 10?*

Here's how I break down a three-year goal:

- **Year 1 – Foundation:** You set the stage, build systems, identify capability gaps, and design for what's coming.
- **Year 2 – Consolidation:** You refine, improve your execution, and hold the line on standards and culture.
- **Year 3 – Acceleration:** You start seeing traction, your revenue increases, your reputation grows, and you gain momentum.

For some businesses, the improvement is steady throughout the three years. For others (and especially in turnaround situations), it's slow to begin in Year 1, with heavier investment coming in Year 2. All business are different, and it depends on where you start; but it's important to know that wherever you're starting is okay. Ultimately, the message is the same for every business: you do it your way. This is not a paint-by-numbers exercise; you're designing and painting your masterpiece, brushstroke by brushstroke, your way.

The future belongs to those who think bigger

Thinking bigger is a skill, a discipline, and a practice. And the good news? It's a muscle that strengthens the more you use it. So, dream bigger, plan bolder, and picture yourself 10 years from now, standing at the helm of the business you designed. Then turn back to today and ask: *What's the first brushstroke I need to make?*

In Chapter 4, we shift from bold vision to structured momentum, the practical next step in the Business System component of the Success System. We'll break it down into the one-year game plan, 90-day campaigns, incorporating rocks, and weekly check-ins. These are the core tools that help you turn big goals into real-world, week-by-week progress. This is where clarity meets cadence, and it's how great businesses create rhythm, focus, and accountability across the team.

CHAPTER 4

FROM VISION TO REALITY

THE DISCIPLINE OF EXECUTION

Th
here's a moment that comes for every business owner – usually after a powerful planning session or retreat – when the ideas are fresh, the possibilities feel endless… and then Monday morning hits. Emails, clients, fire drills. And those great ideas? They get filed away in the 'I'll get to it later' folder, never to be seen again. I call this the **execution gap**.

In this chapter, we move from planning to doing, and from the clouds to the ground. Because no matter how inspiring your 10-year horizon may be, or how sharp your strategy, nothing changes unless something gets done. This is the turning point in our journey together – it's where clarity meets commitment.

Picking up the brush

By now, you've defined your legacy, you've clarified your values and the business reputation you want to build, you've stretched your imagination to chart a 10-year horizon and translated that into a three-year goal. You've done some big and hard thinking.

But let's go back to the metaphor I shared in Chapter 1, which was about painting a new masterpiece over your existing canvas. We can have great ideas and aspirations for our business's future, but the brushstrokes don't apply themselves. So, this chapter is all about action – intentional, strategic, and sustained action – that can bring your plans to life.

Tethering to the future

Most businesses make the mistake of tethering their plans to where they are today. If you plant the same seeds in the same soil every year, you'll grow the same crop, no matter how much you wish for something different. To harvest a new future, you have to change what you plant and sometimes even where you plant it. New outcomes start with new thinking.

When your planning and decision-making are driven by your 10-year horizon, and not by your current constraints or thinking, you unlock momentum. It's not easy, but it's *uplifting*. That future vision becomes your gravity, and it starts pulling you forward. This is how we make the shift from a present-bound mindset to a future-led one.

From 10 years to three years to one year

To execute well, we need to zoom in on our current reality, without losing the long view. Start with your 10-year horizon, then ask: *If we're aiming for this vision over the next 10 years, what must we do in the next three to set the course?* This then becomes your **three-year goal**, and it lays the foundation for 12 smaller, more manageable 90-day campaigns.

This 12-quarter thinking represents three years of structured, purposeful movement, as outlined earlier in the three-year goal.

In the first four quarters, you're laying the groundwork to set up systems, structure, people, and clarity.

In the second four quarters, you're refining and strengthening, testing assumptions, and tightening systems.

In the final four quarters, you gain real traction. Business growth becomes scalable, and your business begins to feel entirely different.

Unfortunately, though, too many owners skip the foundation work and try to leap straight into growth. Countless businesses get stuck under the entrepreneurial ceiling and don't break through. Growth doesn't happen instantly – after all, you can't scale chaos. But if you take the time, you can build it right and transform your business into a sustainable and scalable business model.

The one-year game plan

This first year is your foundation year, but each year you should revisit this process. Think of it as the deep groundwork phase of a major construction project. It doesn't look glamorous from the outside, but it's where future growth is made possible. Resist the urge to overpack this year. You need to prioritise what matters most, launch your strategy, and build well. You'll have time to grow and accelerate later.

For your 10-year horizon, your three-year goal, and your one-year game plan, a useful approach is to set goals across six categories: revenue, your premiership list (a high-performance team that could vie for the number one position in your industry), delivery excellence, brand promise, channels to market, and competitive advantage.

When setting goals for revenue, it's important to keep it realistic, as growth is gradual. For example, don't overestimate the first year when you'll still be building systems. Setting goals for your premiership list encourages you to think about who you will need to bring on as you scale, and to consider which roles will come first. When thinking about delivery and brand promise, set goals related to consistency in delivery and how you can embed your values into the business culture. Considering channels to market encourages you to set goals around targeting markets to extend your reach and align with your future direction. And finally, goals around competitive advantage get you thinking about what sets you apart, what makes your business different, and how you can protect your edge.

Rocks and the power of 90-day campaigns

One of the most powerful tools in the Accelerate system is the concept of rocks – an idea borrowed from Stephen Covey – which are the top strategic priorities you commit to for each 90-day period, to help you achieve the one-year game plan, three-year goals, and the 10-year horizon.

The concept of rocks comes from Covey's classic metaphor: if you fill a jar with sand and pebbles first, then try to add larger rocks, they won't fit. But if you place the rocks in the jar first, you can pour the pebbles and sand in around them. In our businesses, the rocks are the big things we're focusing on, while the pebbles and sand represent the things that come at us in the day-to-day, which consume our time and focus. If we spend too much time on the pebbles and sand, we won't have the resources or bandwidth for important long-term priorities.

Ideally, each quarter, you'll set new rocks and run a structured session with the team and key stakeholders. This model, which has been adapted from *Traction* by Gino Wickman, creates a structured process to identify key priorities and build momentum:

1. List current issues.
2. Identify your most important priorities.
3. Brainstorm solutions.
4. Choose your rocks for the next 90 days.
5. Plan how to track the rocks weekly.

These five points make up the core agenda for your meeting. The process gets your team on the same page, the rocks keep you focused, and planning the tracking ensures you maintain momentum and stay the course.

12-quarter thinking

While the rocks and 90-day campaigns are vital, I'm a huge fan of 12-quarter thinking because it balances vision and practicality. Rather than thinking about each quarter in isolation, considering the cumulative efforts of 12 quarters over three years encourages business owners to align their short-term goals to their three-year game plan.

Using 12-quarter thinking grounds your vision in metrics and momentum, in clear categories. This clarity gives you a map for what to do *and when.*

Case study: 12-quarter thinking

I once worked with a fourth-generation meat-processing business, a stalwart of its region. They'd been around for over a century, and were known for quality, consistency, and strong family values. But like many mature businesses in traditional industries, they'd hit a ceiling. Growth was often spoken about like a pipe dream, something that might happen if the stars aligned or a big contract fell into their lap. The market fluctuated greatly, competition was fierce, and margins were paper thin.

That's when we introduced **12-quarter thinking**. It was a total shift in mindset, from managing the week-to-week chaos to building a clear, intentional roadmap for the next three years. The vision was bold: to break into export markets and become globally competitive. Not by chance, but by design. We mapped out what needed to be true 12 quarters from now – including international certifications, modern traceability systems, a sharper brand, deeper leadership capability – and then worked backwards, one quarter at a time. The leaders didn't try to fix everything at once, but quarter by quarter, they unlocked capability. One quarter focused on upgrading quality assurance processes, another was about entering trade networks, and a later quarter was focused on developing the next layer of management.

Over these 12 quarters, the transformation was profound. They had previously been a business that had accepted flat growth as 'the way it is', but they started to scale in revenue and in belief. Longtime team members were leading improvement projects, the leadership team was forecasting rather than firefighting, and by the ninth quarter, they were landing contracts in the Middle East, had increased throughput by 300%, and were known in the region as a benchmark business. This wasn't luck; it was focus. They stopped dreaming about growth and started building it, one quarter at a time. In a sector where growth was rare, this business proved that maturity doesn't mean stagnation – it means you need a different way to think forward.

Why execution fails

Harvard Business School Professor John Kotter famously reported that 70% of change efforts fail. But let's be honest: most business owners don't fail because of bad ideas... They fail because execution breaks down. Some of the most common blockers to execution of plans that I see are:

- **Overwhelm** (where the business owner and/or leaders have too many competing priorities)
- **Perfectionism** (owners waiting to get it 'just right')
- **Avoidance** (there can be a fear of failure or judgment)
- **Urgency addiction** (mistaking busyness for progress and spending too much time in the weeds)
- **Lack of time** (not protecting or prioritising rocks and strategic imperatives).

As a business owner, I get it. I've lived all those challenges, and I've learned the hard way that execution isn't about hustle – it's about structure.

Overwhelm

Overwhelm is one of the most common roadblocks to execution, especially for founders and leaders wearing multiple hats. When everything feels urgent, nothing gets the focused attention it deserves. The default mode becomes reaction rather than intention, and strategic priorities – those 'important but not urgent' tasks – get constantly sidelined. This fragmentation drains energy and slows progress.

To combat overwhelm, you need clarity and constraint. Begin by ruthlessly prioritising your top three 'rocks' each quarter – these are your non-negotiable outcomes. Everything else is a distraction unless it directly supports those priorities. Use tools like time-blocking, weekly planning rituals, or daily 'power hours' to create protected space for strategic work. And remember that delegation isn't weakness, it's leadership. If you're overwhelmed, chances are you're still doing things someone else could own. Execution improves not when you do more, but when you focus more.

Perfectionism

Perfectionism masquerades as high standards, but it's often fear in disguise. Many business owners delay decisions, product launches, or system rollouts because they're not 'ready yet'. They want the logo sharper, the wording tighter, the process cleaner; but perfection is an illusion, and waiting for it creates inertia.

Execution isn't about getting it perfect; it's about getting it going. Start scrappy, learn fast, and iterate. Think MVP – minimum viable product – because when you get something into the world, you gain real feedback, momentum, and confidence. Done is always better than perfect, especially in a fast-moving environment.

To overcome perfectionism, shift your focus from outcomes to learning. Ask: What's the next testable action? What's the smallest thing I could ship that still adds value? Encourage this mindset in your team too and normalise progress over polish. A bias for action builds culture, and culture builds traction.

Avoidance

Avoidance often stems from a deeper fear of getting it wrong, of being judged, or of exposing a perceived weakness. Business owners might know what needs to be done, but still find themselves stalling, procrastinating, or endlessly re-planning instead of executing. This creates a cycle of guilt and delay.

The key is naming what you're avoiding, and why. Is it a conversation you've been dreading? A system you don't fully understand? A step that makes you feel out of your depth? Get curious, not critical, then break it down into smaller, less threatening actions, and take the first imperfect step. Remember the saying 'How do you eat an elephant? One bite at a time'.

Accountability helps too. Share your intentions with a peer, coach, or team member, because when the task lives only in your head, avoidance is easy. On the other hand, when it's visible to others, commitment increases. Remember: you don't need to be fearless; you just need to move forward anyway. Clarity follows action, not the other way around.

Urgency addiction

In many businesses, I see a quiet addiction to urgency. It feels good to be busy, to knock out quick wins, to respond immediately – but if you're always reacting, you're never leading. Urgency creates adrenaline, but it doesn't create alignment. You end up working *in* the business, not *on* it.

Breaking this cycle starts with redefining productivity. True progress comes from intentional effort on what matters most – not how many emails you've cleared or meetings you've taken. Create structured planning cycles (for example, weekly, monthly, and quarterly) and revisit your core priorities often. Use tools like the Eisenhower Matrix (from Stephen Covey) to stay anchored, and classify your options as either urgent or not urgent, important or not important. As Covey recommends, focus on the 'important but not urgent' quadrant, which is where your rocks live.

Also, look at what urgency might be covering up. Is it a fear of stillness, a lack of strategy, or unclear roles? Build a culture that rewards proactivity, not just reactivity, and schedule regular 'deep work' time (for yourself and your team) to focus on what moves the needle long-term. The goal isn't to eliminate urgency entirely but to stop letting it run the show.

Lack of time

Time is finite, but most business owners treat it like it's negotiable. Strategic priorities are often the first things to be sacrificed when calendars get crowded. Meetings, client fires, and team interruptions fill the day, leaving no room for real progress or strategic thinking.

The solution isn't more time; it's better time discipline and better prioritisation. Using your rocks, reverse-engineer them into weekly commitments and block that time into your calendar *before* anything else. These blocks must be kept sacred.

The other way you can think about it is to use themes (for example, Monday = Strategy, Friday = Team) to structure your week. Say 'no' more often, and challenge the belief that everything must be done now or by you. You're not short on time – you're short on protected time.

Execution thrives when space is made for it. If your calendar is filled with other people's priorities, your business will never reflect your own. I often hear business owners tell me that they're 'busy', but the reality is, we all have the same amount of time and we're all 'busy'. It's how we prioritise the use of our time that differs.

Effort is the engine

Let's wrap up this chapter with one of my favourite quotes from Carol Dweck, author of *Mindset: The New Psychology of Success*: 'Effort is what ignites ability and turns it into accomplishment.' Don't leave your goals on the shelf, and don't let your dreams collect dust. Pick up the brush, and start the work.

You've got 12 quarters, 90-day campaigns, and weekly check-ins. You have everything you need.

This is the turning point. Up to now, we've been working on your Business System, which is the thinking, the planning, the strategic direction. But from here, we step into your Operating System, which is where the work gets done, value is created, and the business starts to move with purpose and precision. This is where most owners and leaders feel right at home: solving problems, getting things out the door, and keeping the wheels turning.

In Chapter 5, we begin with the first of four core themes of execution: your product. We'll explore what you offer the market, not just in terms of what you make or deliver, but how it's developed, documented, improved, and systemised. Because strong businesses don't just sell, they design, package, and replicate value.

THE POWER OF PRODUCT

CREATING YOUR NICHE AND YOUR MONOPOLY

When people hear the word 'monopoly', they think of the board game or big corporations being broken up by regulators. However, I want to redefine that word for you. In the context of *your* business, monopoly isn't about power, it's about precision. It's about being so distinct in what you offer, and so trusted by the people you serve, that there's simply no viable substitute for what you do. That's not dominance in the marketplace, it's success as a result of your actions. And it starts with your product.

The concept of creating your monopoly to own a market was popularised by Peter Thiel in his book *Zero to One*. If you're not crystal-clear about what you're offering, who it's for, and how it's different, then no amount of execution will help you scale.

Differentiation is the game

Let's begin with a simple rule: If you can't be better, be different. Differentiation in the marketplace is not optional, or something that is merely 'nice to have'. In a world of lookalikes, and multiple solutions to the same problem, being one of many is a losing strategy. If your product or service isn't clearly distinguishable from the next provider, you end up competing on price, and that is a race to the bottom.

In my presentations with business owners on product, I often show an image of an emperor tamarin monkey. As you can see in Figure 3, they have a very distinctive long white moustache, which differentiates them from other monkeys. That little moustache isn't just for style – it's actually a biological marker that helps members of the species distinguish themselves.

Figure 3: Emperor Tamarin Monkey
(image reproduced under creative commons:
https://commons.wikimedia.org/wiki/File:Emperor_Tamarin_SF_ZOO.jpg)

I share the story of the emperor tamarin to get you thinking about what your product's distinctive white moustache is. Your product needs a feature, a value, or a story that makes people instantly recognise it as unique or distinct from that of your competitors.

This is only the first part of the challenge, though, because once you have your point of difference, your job is to carve out your niche. Your goal should be to make yourself not only visible in the market but *essential* to the right market.

Step 1: Create a monopoly

Creating your niche monopoly starts with rejecting the 'red ocean' (as coined by Chan Kim and Renee Mauborgne), which is the crowded, bloody market where everyone fights for a bigger slice of the same pie. The goal, instead, is to find your 'blue ocean'. This is a market space you define, where you don't compete for demand, but instead create it.

A great example of finding the blue ocean is that of Cirque du Soleil. They didn't try to build a better circus to compete with what was already out there – they redefined what a circus could be.

The same principle applies to you and the product or service you're putting out to the world. If you're doing what everyone else is doing, your product or service is interchangeable with any other on the market. When that happens, price becomes the only differentiator, and when you become a price taker, all profits are competed away. But when you create a blue ocean, you make yourself indispensable and irreplaceable. You often attract a price premium, and you have a captive audience for your product or service.

And that's where this definition of 'monopoly' differs: you shouldn't be seeking to dominate an existing market – you should be building one that's yours.

Step 2: Decide how you compete

In every market, there are three dimensions of competition: you can compete on quality, service, and/or price. But there's a catch: you can't compete on all three. Think about it – if you can compete on the quality of the product and the service customers receive, you cannot compete on price. If you are a great option because of your price and quality, your service won't be able to be as good. If you try to compete on all three at the same time, you'll end up diluted, inconsistent, and forgettable.

Big corporations that can produce or purchase product on a large scale can afford to play the price game; but unfortunately you can't. That means your path lies in competing on both quality and service at a level that sets you apart from competitors.

So, what does that look like? It means choosing to be a price setter, not a price taker. It means building a business where your clients pay *your* prices – because you offer something they can't get anywhere else. It is about having a value proposition so compelling that you can name your price.

But how do you do that? You have to build systems that ensure every interaction with customers is consistently excellent, and you make strategic choices about who you serve and how. Your product and service need to be exceptional, systems driven, quality assured and consistent. If they are, your customers will pay.

Step 3: Build the system

Differentiating yourself in the market isn't just about the idea or specifics of a product, it's about repetition. A great product offered inconsistently is a failed promise – so that's where systems come in. Your Operating System is the infrastructure that turns your unique value into consistent outcomes. Think of it as the engine behind your monopoly. Good systems allow you to:

- Deliver quality at scale.
- Train others to replicate your best work.
- Monitor performance.
- Adapt as needed, without falling apart.

Organisational theorist and systems thinker Professor Russell Ackoff put it beautifully when he said: 'A system is never the sum of its parts; it's the product of their interactions'. In other words, your system isn't just your procedures and policies, it's how your people interact with those procedures and policies to demonstrate excellence. That's why I often talk about training and coaching as an essential part of your product strategy – if your people don't understand what they need to deliver, or don't possess the capability to deliver it, you're never going to be able to achieve your 10-year horizon.

The trap of loving your product too much

Here's a warning for the passionate entrepreneurs (and I count myself among them): don't fall so in love with your product that you forget to love your customer. American business professional Jay Abraham nailed it when he said, 'Most entrepreneurs fall in love with their product instead of their customer'. While it's important to appreciate what you offer, if you focus on your output too much, you lose sight of the market. You start designing and modifying the product or service for yourself, not for the people you serve.

Ultimately, your goal is not just to build something you're proud of. It's to build something *that your market can't live without*. That's why I encourage all my clients to shift from a product-centric mindset to a customer-centric one. The goal isn't to convince the world to love your creation; rather, it's to create something the world is already asking for, and then deliver it better than anyone else.

Leverage what you know

I often use the following model to help business owners understand the relationship between systems and people capability. It is a powerful visual which emphasises that when we have key person risk, and don't have the systems to facilitate others doing what our key people have traditionally done, it is challenging – if not impossible – to scale. It is only when your business is run by highly capable people and 80% systems driven that you could be considered to exemplify best practice in how you operate.

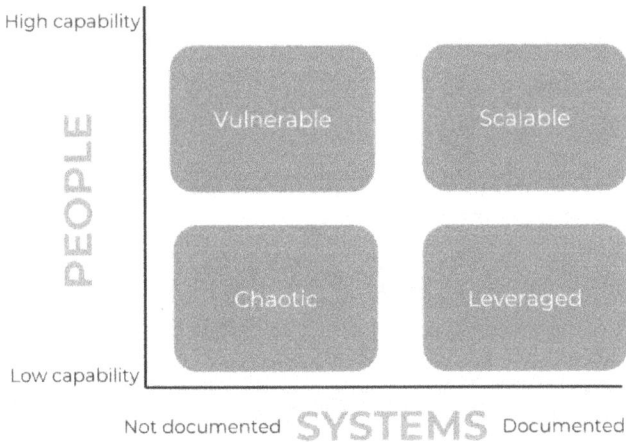

Figure 4: The Leverage Model

Many businesses I work with live in the left side of the model, in the 'chaotic' or 'vulnerable' stages, where the owner is capable but has no systems, or there are minimal systems but no capable team to execute them. To scale, however, you must move to the upper-right quadrant, with high-capability people and high-quality systems.

But there's no straight line to the 'scalable' quadrant from 'chaotic' or 'vulnerable'. You've got to go through the messy middle, and the only way to go up is first to go down. You need to trust others, document what's in your head, and let go of control so your business can grow beyond you. Yes, it's going to feel uncomfortable as you gradually let go, looking for the new systems to impact, but over time the systems will cover you through the leveraged phase and ultimately up to the scalable quadrant.

Case study: Empowering your team

When my client Peter took over the family transport and logistics business from his father, he inherited more than just trucks and depots; he inherited a legacy of hard work, loyalty, and doing whatever it took to get the job done. His dad built the company on sheer determination and personal relationships. If a truck broke down, he'd drive halfway across the state to make the delivery. If a driver called in sick, he'd jump behind the wheel himself. Peter grew up in that world, watching, learning, doing. And for a while, he ran the business the same way: hands-on, always on, solving problems with hustle and know-how.

But as the business grew, Peter started to feel the cracks. Every new contract stretched them. Every extra truck added more complexity. He couldn't be everywhere anymore, and deep down, he knew that the way his dad had run things, though legendary, wasn't sustainable in today's market. That's when he made the call to change not just the business but *himself*. Over time, Peter shifted his identity from being 'the doer' to becoming 'the builder'. He stopped trying to be the smartest guy in the room and started building systems that made the business smarter. He documented what had lived in people's heads for decades. He empowered his team. He held the line on processes, even when it was uncomfortable. And slowly, the business stopped relying on his presence and started running on its own strength.

The results that Peter witnessed and his business experienced were undeniable. With a dependable, repeatable engine underneath, Peter took the business literally into new territory. They expanded interstate, secured contracts with national retailers, and opened a new depot in a growth corridor. Staff turnover dropped, customer retention climbed... And Peter? He wasn't working fewer hours because he cared less; he just didn't have to carry it all alone anymore. His biggest win wasn't just scale and revenue, it was freedom – and that came from choosing to lead differently. By leading with structure rather than heroics, he changed everything.

So, yes, build a monopoly, create a blue ocean, define your niche and own it – but do it in a way that is systems driven, sustainable, quality-assured and free of key person risk.

Continuous improvement: The final ingredient

Once your product is differentiated and your systems are in place, your job isn't done. You now enter the discipline of continuous improvement. This means:

· Regularly reviewing your systems.

· Gathering feedback from clients and team members.

· Benchmarking against industry best practice.

· Innovating without losing focus.

Continuous improvement keeps you sharp and prevents complacency. It ensures that as your market evolves, your product stays relevant and continues to address the needs of your paying customers. It's about staying ahead of the competition while building your reputation, nurturing loyal and engaged customers, and remaining adaptive and responsive to change. So, to tie it all together, here's the cycle we're creating:

1. **Differentiated offering** – Offering the market something that is unique and valuable.

2. **Building capability** – Empowering your team to develop commercial skills while creating systems, procedures, and policies that deliver to a high standard.

3. **Continuous improvement** – Evolving and continuing to learn from your market and your people to stay exceptional.

These three elements interact to create a business that isn't just sustainable, but is magnetic.

In Chapter 6, we move into the second 'P' of the Operating System: people. This is often the area that I spend most time mentoring my clients on – because your systems are only as strong as the humans who use them. And the future of your business depends on who's coming with you.

CHAPTER 6

THE PEOPLE BLUEPRINT

UNLOCKING THE POTENTIAL IN YOUR PEOPLE

The people problem in small and medium-sized businesses often stems from the fact that most business owners end up chained to their own expertise. As a result of being the person who 'knows everything', and without meaning to, you build a team around you that depends on you and your knowledge.

However, real growth happens when you learn to leverage your knowledge and skills so others can do what you once did – and in time, even do it better. This is when your people become an extension of your thinking, carrying your standards into every corner of the business without you needing to stand over them.

You can't control what people do – only how you lead

Before we jump into practical ways to improve this, it's important to accept a tough but freeing truth: you can't control what other people do. Ultimately, you can't control whether your sales team picks up the phone today. You can't control if your site supervisor follows the checklist every single time. You can't control if your draftsperson double-checks every dimension before sending drawings out. But here's what you can control: your actions, your effort, your thinking, and your attitude.

When you focus on what you can control, your leadership becomes proactive rather than reactive. Instead of constantly putting out fires and feeling frustrated, you build systems and processes that empower others to step up. You stop relying on 'hoping' people do the right thing and start designing an environment where the right actions are easier to take. This mindset shift changes everything. The goal is to stop being the bottleneck and start being the architect.

The art of multiplying yourself

If you're like most founders, you started as the best technician in your field, the best welder, the best designer, or the best sales negotiator. But the same skill that helped you build your business and reputation can hold you back when you become the only person trusted to do it right.

A regional manufacturing owner I worked with was in this exact spot. Every custom job still went through him, because he believed no one could weld to his level of precision. But after investing time to document his approach, train his senior fabricators, and create clear visual standards, he saw his top guys begin taking over the most complex builds. They didn't just follow instructions, though; they ended up becoming champions of his approach, upholding his standards even when he wasn't watching.

Within a year, the owner wasn't stuck in the workshop every weekend. Lead times dropped, revenue climbed, and for the first time in years, he took a proper fishing trip without his phone lighting up every hour!

Building thinking, not just tasks

When you want to truly leverage your expertise, you have to move beyond simply handing out tasks, because you need to teach people how to think, and how to make decisions the way you would. This is true delegating, where you give your team every chance of success in completing the task. The opposite of this behaviour is abdicating your leadership responsibility – where you direct your team to undertake a task without the right systems, capability, knowledge, information, or support. Abdicating is a sure-fire way to get dragged back into operations, having to fix mistakes, rescue clients, and deal with warranty issues.

The hidden cost of abdicating your leadership responsibility is the erosion of confidence and trust in your people. When this occurs, and before you know it, you will be back with the 'no one can do it like me' mindset fully entrenched. Scaling your business again becomes a pipe dream as you remain trapped under the entrepreneurial ceiling.

In a project management and engineering consultancy I worked with, senior engineers were constantly stuck approving every design tweak and handling client risk discussion personally. They realised they were simply delegating tasks, not transferring decision-making to the less-experienced engineers.

Consequently, they shifted their approach and started working with junior engineers using guided questions instead of just corrections. These open-ended questions looked something like this:

- 'How would you justify this design choice to the client?'
- 'What risks do you see here, and how would you mitigate them?'
- 'If you were me, what would you prioritise?'

The questions got the junior engineers thinking, and while it took longer upfront to build capacity, it paid off fast. Over time, the junior engineers started operating as trusted operators of the firm's playbook, and they were able to make smart calls on their own. Before long, they were running client workshops confidently, which freed up the senior engineers to focus on growth and innovation of the business.

Ownership over excuses

One of the biggest shifts in turning your team into true extensions of your expertise is getting them to own the outcomes, not just their actions. Think about a real estate principal who constantly worries about whether her agents are following up on leads or keeping vendors informed. She can't force them to make every call, but she can set clear expectations, provide evidence-based feedback, explain the impact, and define the way forward together. Instead of 'You're not doing enough', good feedback becomes:

- 'Here's what we agreed to – 30 calls a week.'
- 'Here's what the data shows – you averaged 12.'
- 'This affects our listing pipeline and market reputation.'
- 'Let's agree on how to get back on track and what support you need.'

This type of clarity and structure invites ownership of the outcomes for the employee rather than excuses. It shows team members exactly how to step up and become champions of your approach, driving results without you micromanaging.

Sharing your standards, not just your skills

Your standards are what set your business apart, whether that's spotless electrical switchboards, bulletproof engineering models, or gold-standard client care in real estate. When standards live inside one person's head, they can't scale. But when they're clearly taught, documented, and reinforced, they spread. Suddenly, your supervisors, project managers, or warehouse leads become extensions of your standards and values, protecting your reputation and freeing you up to work on the business. The standards that you document, teach, and reinforce will completely depend on your industry; but they could include clear quality checklists, training staff in what 'good' or 'excellent' looks like, and actively building a culture where employees are proud of the work they are doing.

Growing future leaders before you need them

Another key people problem I see is where business owners don't actively build future leaders in their company until they need to employ someone. And often at this pinch point they suddenly realise that no one within the organisation has the skills and capability to take on the new role.

Case study: Growing future leaders

A freight and logistics operator that I worked with learned this the hard way when two senior dispatch supervisors resigned back to back. Chaos ensued, routes were delayed, drivers were lost, and customer complaints skyrocketed. This issue primarily occurred because they had no pipeline of trained team leaders ready to step up who were capable of working at that level. As a result of the gap in in-house talent, they started identifying 'nearly ready' leaders, who were people with the potential to operate at the required level in the near future. They invited these emerging leaders to shadow dispatch meetings, learn customer communication scripts, and take the lead on mini projects.

After 12 months, they had a group of dispatch supervisors who were ready, willing, and good enough to take the reins.

The owner said to me, 'They became my arms and legs: and now I finally sleep at night.'

When we build capacity and leadership in our people, the knock-on effect to the business owner is the freedom that comes when others can take the lead and carry forward what we once did alone.

Aspiration: Fuel for the journey

When people stop aspiring, they start checking out; and as business owners and leaders, it's in our interests to help our people identify future aspirations and career paths within our business. We want them to have agency over their career choices and aspirations, but we need to help them find a path for growth and progression.

Many of our younger employees have grown up on video games, where they are rewarded by going through the levels, and watching short snippets of content on social media where the 'next thing' comes very quickly. Similarly, career mapping with multiple levels, divided by short- and medium-term competency gateways, rewards curiosity, learning, and ambition and self-selects those who have greater aspirations.

Career mapping is about three things:

1. **Clear progression** – Show people where they can go and what the steps are.

2. **Competency gates** – Define the skills and milestones that unlock the next level.

3. **Structured development plans** – Outline how you'll help them get there.

When your team can *see* a future inside your business, they're more likely to commit, to care, and to grow with you. And when personal ambition and company vision align? That's where momentum lives.

Same side of the desk

The 'same side of the desk' metaphor is one of my favourites. Too often, leaders and team members face each other like they're negotiating. But real performance and real loyalty come when you sit next to each other, solving the same problem, and aiming for the same goal.

Align your employees' ambition with your business success, become their greatest fan, cheer loudly for them, and will them to the next level. If you can get this right, you'll shift from a transactional leader–employee relationship to a transformational one.

Case study: The turning point in the dairy

For years, Matt ran his family's dairy business the only way he knew how: sleeves rolled up, boots on the ground, calling the shots. He'd inherited the role from his father, and like many in the industry, he believed strong leadership meant giving clear instructions and expecting people to follow him. The cows were milked, the trucks came on time, and the bills got paid. But something was missing, and it was about to get worse before it got better.

The turning point came in the space of six months when three of Matt's most capable team members walked away, all for promotional opportunities elsewhere. One went to a bigger farm with better pay, another into agribusiness sales, and the last into an entirely different industry. What hurt wasn't just losing the people; it was what they said on the way out: 'There's no clear path here.' 'I want to grow, and I can't see how I will.' 'I don't feel seen, Matt. I'm just told what to do.' The feedback landed hard. Matt realised he hadn't built a team; he'd built a roster… and people don't stay on rosters forever.

That's when Matt realised he had to change not just his approach but his mindset. He metaphorically stepped out from behind the desk, not to give orders, but to get on the same side as his team. He started asking questions instead of giving them answers. 'What do you care about?' 'Where do you want to go?' 'What lights you up?' He brought in professional development – not just training, but real curiosity-driven learning. He mapped out a clear career path for each team member, showing them how they could progress, earn more, lead others, and build a future right where they were. He reshaped the structure of the business so there were roles to grow into and rewards for effort – not just for showing up, but for stepping up.

And then the energy shifted: people started leaning in, and new hires came not just for a job but for a journey. Matt stopped being the boss who had all the answers and became the leader who believed in his people's potential. He created a vision that was bigger than the next milking cycle, and it was one that made the team proud to be part of it. Today, the business is thriving, productivity is up, staff retention is strong, and Matt isn't carrying it all on his own anymore. He went from command to collaboration, because he stopped telling and began inspiring; and ultimately he went from running a business to leading a team.

Moving from telling to empowering

When you're flat-out, it's tempting to just tell people what to do and move on. But real leverage happens when you empower your people to figure it out themselves and act without you. This might feel hard to do to begin with, but I'd encourage you to start small. Instead of telling a junior electrician, 'Check the fuse and replace it,' you might ask questions like, 'What do you think is causing the short? How would you diagnose it?'

At first, it is going to feel slow. But you're building their muscle memory and helping them to learn to think and act independently. Over time, your staff will start operating as trusted extensions of your thinking, solving problems before they even reach your desk.

A mechanical design team I worked with started doing this intentionally, and deliberately moved from 'tell' to 'ask' coaching. Their senior drafters taught juniors to challenge assumptions and validate decisions. Within a year, those juniors were running client design meetings and trouble-shooting issues on their own. The seniors finally had the space to focus on complex, high-value projects and research and development (R&D).

Your leadership shifts from reactive to proactive

When you focus on what you can control – your mindset, your communication, your standards, and your systems – you shift your leadership from reactive firefighting to proactive design. You stop saying, 'I hope they do it right,' and start saying, 'I know they'll do it right because I've shown them how to think, I've given them the tools and systems to do it well, and I've built a culture where they take ownership.'

That's when you start seeing real leverage. Your team becomes an extension of your skill set, and you move from working *in* the business to truly working *on* it.

Imagine stepping onto a job site and seeing your supervisors problem-solving confidently, and making judgment calls that match your standards, without you directing every move. Picture your designers handling client calls with the same care and precision as you would, leaving you free to focus on strategy and growth. Visualise your agents listing and selling properties with the same values and service levels, so your reputation only gets stronger while you step back from the day-to-day hustle.

That's the future you're building when you multiply yourself into your team.

Your next move

You don't need to change everything overnight: start small, pick one decision, one piece of technical knowledge, or one process that only lives in your head, and start planning how you'll pass it on. Ask yourself: 'Who could take this on if I invested time to teach them? What systems or training would need to exist to make them successful? How can I support them to think, not just do?'

When you focus on what you can control and invest in empowering others, you transform your business from a people problem machine into a people-powered growth engine. Start multiplying yourself, and watch your business unlock its true potential.

People design your product. People deliver your service. People build your brand. People drive your culture. Therefore, if you want to grow, sure, you need great systems and a great strategy, but you ultimately need people who are committed, equipped, and inspired. If you can get the people piece right, everything else gets easier.

In the next chapter, we turn our attention to promotion, which is how to position what you do, how to attract your ideal customers, and how to make sure your message matches your mission.

CHAPTER 7

PROMOTION WITH PURPOSE

FROM NOISE TO CONNECTION

f there's one part of business that feels endlessly noisy, it's marketing. Ads shout at us, social feeds scroll endlessly, and everyone seems to be fighting to be seen, heard, and chosen. But the truth is, promotion isn't about shouting louder – it's about being clearer in your messaging. The goal isn't to blast a message into the void; the goal is to connect with real people, in meaningful ways, through a message that resonates. Promotion isn't just about selling. It's about alignment. It's about giving your ideal clients a compelling reason to say 'yes' because they feel that you see them, get them, and can help them.

Not everyone is your client

Seth Godin said it best: 'It's impossible to create worth that both matters and pleases everyone.' So, let's stop trying. Not everyone is your client, and that's a relief. You couldn't serve everyone anyway, even if you wanted to! The moment you let go of needing to appeal to everyone is the moment you unlock real power in your marketing; because now you can focus, and you can speak directly to the people who resonate with your values, your offer, and your way of doing business.

That focus starts with five core questions, and every effective promotional strategy I've ever seen has clear answers to these:

1. Who are you talking to?
2. What are you promising?
3. How will you get noticed?
4. How will you inspire a buying response?
5. How will you get them to buy again and again?

These questions aren't theoretical. They form the bones of a marketing system that's repeatable, scalable, and above all, authentic.

Demographics tell you who, psychographics tell you why

Two people can be the same age, have the same job title, and live in the same postcode, but one values status and exclusivity, while the other values sustainability and simplicity. You can't market to them the same way, even though their demographics are similar – and this is where psychographics come in.

Let's take a simple example: the motor car you drive. If we take a poll of 100 people and ask them to nominate their ideal car, each is likely to focus on different elements of the value proposition. Some will need to transport large families, some will want to tow caravans, some will value electric or hybrid cars, as this aligns with their personal values, while others might want to stand out, in which case a McLaren could be just the thing.

Demographics tell you who your customer is – for example, how old they are, where they live, their gender, or what industry they work in (if you ask them these things). But psychographics tell you why they buy. When you understand your client's values, beliefs, interests, and aspirations, you move from marketing based on demographic information to psychographics. This build connection, because your most powerful messages won't just describe your product – they'll reflect your client's identity. That's when your audience starts to feel like you're the only business that truly 'gets them'.

Brand promise: Your market pledge

When you know who you are and who you serve, your brand creates a promise to the market. It's not just a slogan or tagline, but a commitment – your market pledge, if you like. Your brand promise is your consistent declaration of what you'll always deliver, no matter what.

For your brand promise to land authentically with your market, it has to align with your values, your behaviours, and the impact you want to have, as defined in your Eco System. It should speak directly to your customers' values and aspirations. When you hit that sweet spot, you stop being a commodity and you become a trusted, go-to choice.

Craft the conversation

Marketing is a conversation, rather than a campaign; and every great conversation begins with listening. I teach a three-part model to my clients. First, **profile your ideal client**. Get inside their world. Use psychographics to ask: What do they care about? What frustrates them? What motivates them? Next, **identify their pain points**. What's not working for them? Where do they feel stuck, overwhelmed, or behind? Then, **position your offer as the solution**. Frame your product or service not just in terms of features but in terms of feelings: relief, momentum, clarity, growth.

Look at how Apple markets the iPhone. They're not just selling a phone; they're selling simplicity, status, creativity, and lifestyle. Apple understands their ideal customer deeply. Their ads don't list every technical spec; instead, they focus on how the product makes the user feel: more capable, more creative, and more connected.

Apple don't shout into the void. They speak with precision and elegance in specific places. Their brand promise is implicit in everything they do – and it just works, because they've kept that promise consistently over decades. From the product launch videos to their billboard campaigns, everything reinforces the message of premium design, intuitive experience, and innovation that elevates your life. Psychographically, Apple appeal to those who value design, ease, and brand prestige. They aren't targeting every phone buyer. In fact, they deliberately exclude many by positioning themselves at the top end of the market.

And that's the lesson: clarity in the problem your product solves, for a very specific market that truly values the offer and is willing to pay for the solution, beats volume. To do this successfully, you have to know your client, speak their language, and deliver on your promise with intention and consistency. When you frame your marketing this way, your audience feels seen, heard, and understood. That's emotional resonance, and that's how trust is built.

The four questions for great promotion

Great marketing stands out because it connects. Once you've crafted your message, test it against these four questions:

1. Is it **empathetic**? Does it show your audience you understand them deeply?
2. Is it **distinct**? Does it make clear why you're the only choice?
3. Is it **visible**? Will the right people actually see it?
4. Does it **matter**? Does it create urgency and relevance?

If your current marketing is falling flat, one of these four is probably missing. And this is your cue to adjust.

Farming and hunting: The twin engines of growth

In your promotional mix, there are two core strategies: farming and hunting.

Farming (often referred to as marketing) is a structured way to position in a broader market, wait for your audience to emerge, build trust and social proof, then harvest the sale. It's a process that identifies and qualifies genuine prospects: clients you want, with the means and desire to commit. It's slow and steady to win the race and often results in extraordinary lifetime value, signified by repeat business and genuine advocacy. Done well, you create raving fans as you build long-term trust.

Hunting (often referred to as sales), on the other hand, is a much more direct approach and can bolster sales fast. You have your primary targets, which I call your 'love list'. You track them, you court them, you engage with them in a very deliberate way and close the deal. In this fascinating game of continuous improvement, reviews of craft and tactics are critical as the prey gets wilier and the hunter never stops learning.

Farming is about nurturing existing relationships, educating, and it's slow and steady. It's the strategy of long-term trust. Hunting, on the other hand, is more direct. It's bold and intentional, and it keeps your pipeline full.

Farming	Hunting
You plant by educating your audience.	You create your love list of those you wish to work with.
They emerge and you qualify and engage your leads.	You track them and hang out where they hang out.
	You track the right people.
You fertilise using evidence and social proof.	You engage with purpose.
You fertilise by delivering value consistently.	You close with clarity.
	You celebrate and learn.
You harvest and convert these relationships into revenue.	

You need to be proficient in both farming and hunting, but most business owners default to one or the other. However, the real power play is in doing both at the same time. That's how you create both short-term wins and long-term growth.

Storytelling: Your secret weapon

Stories explain. Stories connect. And stories sell. A great story is the bridge between your product and your customer's heart. You don't need Hollywood production. You need real stories that connect and create emotions that prospects can relate to. Think of stories you could share that reflect a transformation achieved by one of your clients, a moment that explains your 'why', a peek behind the scenes into your world, or an insight or win that was unexpected.

Stories stick because they make people feel; and when your clients feel, your brand sticks.

The 35% that matter most

Let me save you some time, stress, and second-guessing: not everyone is going to buy from you. And you know what? That's not a problem. In fact, it's perfectly normal.

There's a brilliant insight from marketing legend Jay Abraham, where he talks about the natural breakdown of every market. He states that only 5% of your possible market are ready to buy right now. This group has already made up their mind, they've done the research, they're hunting for the right option, and if you're in front of them, they'll consider you. If you're not, they'll go somewhere else. Simple.

Then there's about 60% who will never buy from you. No matter how many discounts you offer, how good your product is, or how lovely your logo looks, they're just not your customer. And that's okay.

So, what's left?

That sweet, juicy 35% in the middle. They're your opportunity, because these people haven't made up their mind yet. In fact, many of them haven't even heard of you. But they could buy from you – if you get it right. These are the people you need to focus your marketing energy on. Let me give you an example.

Picture this – you run one of the leading jet ski companies in the world. You've got a killer product, you've got stock in the showroom, the sun's coming out, and you know summer's going to be big. Where are the 5%? They're already pulling into your driveway with a deposit in hand. They've made the decision; now it's about the experience they have with your staff and their execution.

What is happening with the 60%? Honestly, there will be infinite reasons why they're in this group. Maybe they don't live near water, they hate the sound of engines, they travel too much for work to justify the spend, or they just don't do 'fun'. Whatever it is, you're not going to change them.

But the 35%? They're thinking:

- 'Gee, it'd be great to do something adventurous with the kids this summer.'
- 'We've been talking about buying a jet ski for a couple of years.'
- 'I'm sick of working every weekend – I want something that gives us a bit of fun back.'

They're curious. They're imagining. They're halfway there. But they don't know you… yet. So, your job is to show up in their world. Start telling stories about what life looks like with your product. Don't talk about the features; instead, talk about the feeling. Show the young family loading up the trailer on a Friday afternoon. Show the couple exploring a quiet beach with no one around. Show the guy who used to work weekends finally laughing out loud as he skips across the waves.

In other words, speak to where they're at – not where you wish they were. You don't have to win everyone; you just have to win a few more of that 35%. And when you do, your business will start to shift gears.

So, if you're spending your marketing budget trying to convince people who were never going to buy – or if you're only talking to people who were always going to buy: pause, refocus, and go after the moveable middle. Because that's where your next growth opportunity lives.

From pipeline to wallet share

Once someone becomes a customer, the journey isn't over. Now it's about deepening the relationship. This is where wallet share comes in. Don't just aim to win one sale – your goal should be to become their go-to for everything that you offer.

Think value-stacking, personalisation, and meaningful follow-up. If you can do this well, you can transform your customers into raving superfans. And do you know the best part about this? The subsequent sales are easier. You've already done the hard part, which was earning their trust in the first place… Now you get to build on it.

Promotion with purpose

Purposeful promotion is about more than visibility; it's about resonance. It's about:

- Aligning your message with your business Eco System.
- Knowing your ideal client intimately.
- Making a brand promise you keep.
- Blending farming and hunting strategies.
- Telling stories that move people.
- Focusing on the right moveable middle.
- Earning more from the relationships you already have.

Promotion is the third 'P' of the Operating System. It's where your ideas come alive through messaging that lands and offers that convert. In our next chapter, we'll talk about the fourth 'P': Profit. Because your purpose deserves to be funded. Let's make it happen.

CHAPTER 8

PROFIT

UNLOCKING POSSIBILITY

genuinely believe that profit isn't just a financial outcome; it's the fuel for your business's purpose. When I ask business owners what money represents to them, I hear answers like security, opportunity, freedom, time, and rest. Whatever money means to you, profit is the mechanism that unlocks more of what you want.

This chapter is about understanding and improving profit – not just in theory, but through practical, tangible levers you can pull in your business, starting today. Whether you're new to your numbers or already financially fluent, this is where the game gets serious. Because if your business isn't profitable, it can't be sustainable. And if it's not sustainable, you can't keep doing the work that matters most.

Let's create possibility

A client once shared with me that before building a profit-focused mindset, she always saw money as a survival tool – and consequently a source of stress. But when we reframed profit as possibility, not greed, something shifted in her. She realised that sustainable profit gave her the ability to pay her team better, work fewer weekends, and finally take a holiday without guilt. Her profit didn't just give her money; it gave her options and improved her lifestyle.

Yet so many business owners carry beliefs about money that undermine their growth. That's why I like to start with your money mindset; and if you need to read the following line a couple of times, please do:

Profit is not greed. Profit is possibility.

Three beliefs that shift the game

There are three foundational beliefs I encourage every business owner to adopt:

1. Revenue is not profit

To put it bluntly, just because you made a sale, doesn't mean you made money. The costs associated with that sale matter, and understanding your expenses is non-negotiable. I worked with a consulting agency that boasted about $3.2 million in revenue. But when we looked at their books, they were barely breaking even. Why? Because they had bloated delivery costs and inefficient systems. But once they understood the distinction between revenue and profit, they redesigned their pricing model, tracked the costs that made an impact, and profitability followed.

2. Profit is not cash

You can have a healthy profit and loss statement with a strong reported net profit and still be in a cash crisis. A business I mentored hit their quota of throughput and billable work targets for the quarter but couldn't make payroll because their invoicing cycle lagged behind their expenses. Until they built out a reliable cash-flow forecast, systematised their invoicing procedures, and tightened payment terms, their 'profit' as reflected in their bank account remained elusive.

3. Tax money is not your money

I've seen too many business owners celebrate a great quarter, spend freely, and then panic at tax time. Something I do in my own practice, and I advocate for every business owner to adopt, is to have a second bank account for 'tax'. Each paid invoice, each week, or each fortnight, transfer a percentage of revenue into this account, so it's there when the tax bill comes in. For many business owners that I've worked with, this small habit changes everything. Where possible, I like to nominate a set percentage, say 30% of the invoice, to put aside every time a payment is received. This account should be able to cover all your tax obligations, so you're not lying awake in bed at night wondering where you'll find the money (or getting into debt with the tax department).

These three beliefs lay the foundation for clear-eyed decision-making. Once you see profit clearly, you can build it intentionally.

The sand filter analogy

Your business is a bit like a sand filter on a swimming pool. Revenue flows in at the top like water, but before it reaches the bottom as profit, it filters through multiple layers of cost – such as cost of goods sold (COGS), labour, rent, admin, and marketing – and each layer catches some of that water.

Even a small tweak in each layer has the potential to dramatically increase the amount that reaches the bottom. And that's what profit optimisation is about: it's not a total overhaul, but making strategic improvements in small areas, which cumulatively create big changes and improvements.

The 10 levers of profit

Through the Accelerate program, I walk business owners through 10 core financial levers that influence profit, which fall into the following two categories:

1. **Financial management:**
   - Pricing
   - Volume
   - Suppliers
   - Cost of goods sold (COGS)
   - Labour efficiency
   - Overheads

2. **Working capital:**
   - Accounts receivable
   - Accounts payable
   - Inventory
   - Access to capital

The profit game involves focusing on and pulling different levers at different times.

Financial management levers

Pricing is one of the most powerful levers, and one of the most underused strategies for improving profit. We want to raise prices strategically, by communicating value, not just cost. Importantly, you don't need to be a luxury brand to charge more – you just need to deliver better or more value. To do this, think about the following:

· **Value-based:** Charge based on results and outcomes, not inputs like time.

· **Competitive:** Align with market rates.

· **Cost-plus:** Add markup to your cost of goods or materials.

· **Penetration:** Price low to enter a new market.

One thing you may have noticed about each of the above pricing models is that they all serve a specific strategic purpose. It is critical that you are clear on what you are looking to achieve in setting your prices and that you adopt the most appropriate pricing model to serve your strategic purpose.

Ron Baker famously said, 'Profit is the applause you get for creating value.' Yet for many business owners, raising prices feels uncomfortable, like charging more without giving more. This tension often clashes with their personal values and the promises they make to customers. But when price increases are backed by genuine value, improved outcomes, or a better customer experience, they strengthen your brand rather than harming it.

Business owners often tell me that they are reluctant to raise prices in case it leads to lost customers, and this is something that many are not prepared to risk. While this is certainly a possibility, and I understand their concerns, in my experience it rarely occurs.

But what if we came at this pricing issue from a different angle or a whole new paradigm? Rather than increasing prices carte blanche, what if we examined our pricing model in relation to the markets we are serving or – just as importantly – not serving? In examining markets, this would mean thinking about customers and prospects who truly value what we offer, and those who really understand our value proposition and have the means to pay. Identifying these markets will allow us to position ourselves in a way that demonstrates significant value in order to charge a price premium.

A business can command a price premium by clearly aligning its offering with high-value outcomes for its customers. For example, one of my clients ran a consultancy business supporting avocado growers, a sector known for its unpredictability and weather sensitivity. By demonstrating a consistent ability to lift crop yields despite these challenges, they built trust and credibility within the industry. Leveraging this reputation, they successfully expanded into adjacent markets like nuts and table grapes, where similar yield optimisation challenges existed. Because they could show growers the direct link between their services and the potential for significantly increased returns, they were able to confidently raise their prices and position their offering as a value-generating investment rather than a cost, justifying a premium that clients were willing to pay.

There are many effective ways to drive revenue growth, and one of the most accessible is increasing sales to existing customers. This is often the lowest-hanging fruit, as customers already trust you and understand your value. The focus here is on making it easier for them to buy more, more often. By removing friction, introducing logical add-ons, and proactively identifying unmet needs, you can lift volume without needing to chase new markets or leads. You can do this in a number of ways: think loyalty programs, referral bonuses, upsells, limited-time offers, bundled products, and strategic partnerships. If someone is already buying from you, there's capacity to sell them more than what they originally came for, if you provide a compelling value proposition.

While increasing revenue is a powerful way to boost profit, it's just one piece of the puzzle. Sustainable profitability comes from understanding and optimising a broader set of levers that influence your bottom line. These include pricing strategy, volume, cost of goods sold, overheads, productivity, capacity utilisation, working capital, and financial efficiency. When used together, these levers give business owners far more control, not just over revenue, but over margins, cash flow, and long-term financial health. Let's explore how each one can be used to build a stronger, more profitable business.

While revenue growth is an essential lever, true profitability comes from managing what happens beneath the top line, starting with your cost of goods sold (COGS). This includes all the direct costs involved in delivering your product or service – typically materials and production labour. It's a variable cost that scales with revenue, and the gap between revenue and COGS, your gross profit, is one of the most important indicators of financial health. It's also a powerful benchmarking tool to compare your business with industry norms. Improving your gross margin can often deliver more impact than chasing new sales.

To reduce COGS without compromising on quality, businesses should focus on sourcing smarter, negotiating better supplier terms, reducing material waste, and refining internal production systems. One small manufacturing company I worked with achieved a 60% reduction in customer warranty returns simply by strengthening their quality-control processes. This not only minimised rework and waste but also freed up production capacity and lifted overall profitability. Similarly, production labour costs can be improved by increasing workforce efficiency, training staff well, simplifying and standardising repeatable tasks, investing in tools or software that save time, and fostering a culture of accountability and continuous improvement.

Once you've optimised gross profit by managing revenue and COGS, the next key lever is your fixed costs, often referred to as overheads. These are the costs your business incurs regardless of how much you produce or sell – things like rent, insurance, admin salaries, utilities, and software subscriptions. Even if your business made no revenue for a month, these costs would still need to be covered. That's why managing overheads is critical to improving profitability and building financial resilience.

Overheads are unique in that they don't directly fluctuate with sales volume, which means they offer a powerful opportunity to improve margins through economies of scale. As you grow, your fixed costs are spread over a larger revenue base, effectively lowering your cost per unit and increasing your profit margin, provided you keep those overheads in check. However, this benefit doesn't happen automatically. Overheads must be actively managed, and the most effective tool for doing that, regardless of business size, is a budget. A clear, well-structured budget gives visibility, accountability, and control. It allows you to plan ahead, monitor spending, and make informed decisions before issues escalate. In one session I had with a founder, we identified they were paying $800 per month for software they hadn't used in over a year. By cancelling the subscription, we added $9600 in profit to their annual figures.

Reducing overheads doesn't always mean cutting; it's about making smarter choices. That could include stream-lining office space, reviewing underutilised subscriptions, outsourcing non-core functions, or investing in systems that reduce manual administration. By approaching overheads with discipline and strategy, you don't just reduce costs; you unlock capacity, improve cash flow, and strengthen your financial foundations.

With revenue, COGS, and overheads under control, you're in a strong position to start leveraging other profit levers in order to scale with confidence and clarity.

Working capital levers

The accounts receivable lever relates to getting paid as quickly as possible for the work you've done (or work you're doing). Invoice promptly, make it easy to pay, automate reminders, and follow up consistently. One service business I worked with cut their receivable days in half by changing from monthly to weekly invoicing. It's far more beneficial for your business to be holding the cash rather than the business that owes you money. Your business is not a bank.

On the other hand, my advice for accounts payable is the opposite! Stretch payment terms strategically to pay towards the end of the payment window, schedule payments after cash comes in, and negotiate terms where necessary. Don't withhold payments; pay them by the due date. But it makes more sense for the cash to be in your pocket until it needs to be paid out.

One of the most common questions business owners ask when reviewing their annual financials is: 'If I made all this profit, why isn't it showing up in my bank account?' The answer usually lies in where the cash is tied up. It's not uncommon for healthy profits on paper to be offset by poor cash flow in practice. In many businesses, particularly in service, retail, and manufacturing, cash gets trapped in debtors (accounts receivable), inventory, or work in progress (WIP) that hasn't yet been invoiced. In service businesses, WIP can accumulate when work has been done but not billed promptly. For product-based businesses, cash often sits on the shelves in the form of raw materials, parts, or finished goods waiting to be sold. Until that stock is converted into a sale, and more importantly, collected as cash, it's not helping your bank balance. With your inventory, implement 'just-in-time' strategies where possible. Don't let cash gather dust by sitting in stock in the warehouse.

This is why stock turns – how many times you sell and replace inventory in a year – are a key indicator in retail and manufacturing. Low stock turns usually mean excess inventory, tying up working capital and increasing the risk of obsolescence. Obsolete stock or WIP that's too old to sell or invoice becomes a silent killer of profitability, often only uncovered during stocktakes or audits. That's why business owners must stay on top of inventory movement, ageing reports, and billing cycles. It's not just a finance task, it's an operational discipline.

Take the example of a large original equipment manufacturer (OEM) I worked with, which had over $750,000 in obsolete components sitting on shelves – they were mostly parts tied to discontinued product lines or parts that had been superseded by newer designs. Not only was this dead weight on their balance sheet, but it also clogged up valuable warehouse space and distorted their true working capital position. In my work with the owners, we implemented a strategic review, cleared out redundant stock through secondary markets and re-manufacturing initiatives, and tightened forecasting and ordering processes moving forward. Within 12 months, they had turned a stagnant cost centre into a lean, responsive inventory system, freeing up over $500,000 in working capital and improving cash flow significantly.

In short, profit doesn't equal cash. Business owners must actively manage the working capital cycle – especially accounts receivable, WIP, and inventory – to ensure the business has the liquidity it needs to grow, invest, and stay resilient. Staying on top of these areas is a hallmark of a financially resourceful business.

Finally, access to capital is where you build your creditworthiness, understand your debt capacity, and avoid funding through last-minute loans. If this is you, however, build relationships before you need funding, and secure the funding before it becomes urgent.

Triple 5 and Triple 10

I am sure that many business owners reading this could lean on these ideas and pull multiple levers to powerful effect. One of my favourite examples is the power of compounding small changes and how the levers work together to produce extraordinary results. Let me demonstrate. Let's say if your business can

- increase sales by 5%,
- reduce production costs by 5%, and
- reduce overheads by 5%,

this combination can increase your profit uplift by 45% from the previous year. It's what I call the Triple 5 effect.

Similarly, if you stretch each change to 10%, then the result is a 90% uplift in the amount of profit. That's Triple 10.

These numbers aren't just theoretical. I've seen this play out in businesses of every size and sector, from small to medium enterprises to significant manufacturing firms. The key is to start small, track your data, and compound the wins.

You don't need to do everything

Let's be clear, you don't need to overhaul your entire business overnight; but you do need to act. I'd suggest you pick two or three levers that make the most sense right now and integrate them into your quarterly priorities. Profit grows when you build it intentionally – lever by lever, quarter by quarter.

Understanding the financial levers available – like revenue, COGS, overheads, and working capital – is essential, but knowing *which* lever to pull is only part of the equation. To truly take control of your business performance, you need visibility. You need to be able to see where the business is right now, where it's trending, and whether the actions you're taking are actually driving the outcomes you want. This is where data and reporting become critical.

Financial clarity equals business control. Without it, you're making decisions in the dark. Financial literacy isn't just about reading spreadsheets or handing off the numbers to your accountant; rather, it's about aligning your financial reporting with your business strategy. When your numbers speak to your goals, you can assess what's working, course-correct quickly, and make informed decisions that drive momentum.

Core financial statements

If you want to lead your business with confidence and control, there are six key reports you need to understand and track consistently. These reports provide the insights that tell you if your strategy is gaining traction, where the bottlenecks are, and what to prioritise next. When reviewed together, they form the dashboard for strategic financial leadership, not just bookkeeping.

As Warren Buffet famously said, 'The rear vision mirror is always much clearer than the windshield.' So, with that in mind, let's walk through each of these six reports and how to use them to interpret performance, guide your decisions, and move your business forward.

1. **Profit and loss (P&L)** – Shows income and expenses over time. Think of it as the movie of your business performance.
2. **Balance sheet** – Shows assets versus liabilities. It's like a photograph that shows your equity position at a specific point in time.
3. **Cash-flow forecast** – Predicts incoming and outgoing cash. It's your financial weather radar. This is a key element to achieving financial piece of mind. You know what's coming and you can proactively do something about it.
4. **Budget vs actuals** – Compares what you planned versus what actually occurred.
5. **Debtors (accounts receivable)** – Tracks what clients owe you.
6. **Creditors (accounts payable)** – Tracks what you owe others.

When a business owner knows their numbers and what's in these reports, they stop flying blind. They lead with confidence, and they are able to make faster, better decisions.

Profit is not the endgame, it's the enabler

You started this journey with a vision. You've built your Eco System, designed your Business System, and refined your Operating System. Profit is the final piece, and it's important because it sustains everything else.

Profit lets you reinvest in your team. It lets you serve more clients. It lets you take time off, pay yourself well, and build a business that fuels your personal and professional legacy.

So yes, make money. Not for money's sake, but because it's the oxygen that powers your mission. The arena is yours now. Stay bold, stay intentional, and remember: business doesn't have to be by default. You get to build it by design.

Conclusion

A Business Worth Leading

You've now walked through the core elements of building a business by design, piece by piece, system by system, decision by decision. You've looked up and out to define your vision. You've looked inward to clarify your values and your legacy. You've looked outward to define your niche, your message, your impact. And you've looked forward to create a rhythm of execution that aligns strategy with action.

But here's the truth: transformation doesn't come from information. It comes from implementation. Reading this book may have sparked ideas, shifts in mindset, or 'aha' moments – and I hope it did. But the work begins now. The canvas is standing in front of you, the brush is in your hand, and the masterpiece you're building will be created one stroke at a time.

Business isn't built in a burst. It's built in the rhythm of 90-day sprints, steady weekly actions, and patient momentum. There's no doubt that you'll make mistakes along the way; but you'll shift direction, try something new, learn, and that's part of the process. You are building something resilient, and something that can grow without burning you out.

And as you build, never forget why you started.

You didn't come this far just to survive. You started your business because you believed in something, because you saw a better way, and because you wanted to create value, opportunity, freedom, or impact – on your terms. And that's what this journey is really about.

It's not just about more revenue or more clients. It's about more contribution, and more meaning. You're building a business that serves you, your team, and your community; one that is aligned with who you are, and the legacy you want to leave. So, stay committed to the brushstrokes, pick your rocks, lead your people, focus your time, adjust your levers, and celebrate your wins.

And when the chaos creeps in (as it no doubt will) come back to this truth: you're not doing business by accident. You're building it by design. Keep going. You've got this.

Afterword

An Invitation to Continue the Journey

As you close the final pages of this book, I want to thank you for investing your time and energy into exploring new ways to think about and grow your business. Ideas are powerful, but it's in the *implementation* that real transformation happens.

That's exactly why I created Accelerate – a program designed to take the principles and frameworks you've discovered here and turn them into practical steps that drive results using my proprietary success map. It's about bridging the gap between insight and action, giving you the clarity, tools, and support to make lasting change in your business.

If you've found value in these pages, Accelerate will help you embed the learnings, build momentum, and create sustainable growth with confidence.

Beyond Accelerate, there are plenty of other ways we can connect:

- Visit chrisgreen.au to explore a wide range of free business resources, tools, videos, and articles to support your aspirations.
- Subscribe to my podcast to gain further weekly insights in an easily digested and entertaining format.
- Follow me on LinkedIn, where I post a weekly video discussing and unpacking the conversations I am having with business owners everyday.
- Reach out (chris@chrisgreen.au) if you'd like to explore more tailored support. I always enjoy hearing business owners' stories and exploring what's possible together.

This doesn't have to be the end of your journey – it can be the beginning of your next chapter. I'd love to continue supporting you as you turn these ideas into action and build the business you've imagined.

Kind regards

Chris Green

References

Abraham, J. (n.d.). *Marketing strategies and insights.*

Ackoff, R. L. (n.d.). *System thinking insights.*

Brown, B. (2012). *Daring greatly: How the courage to be vulnerable transforms the way we live, love, parent, and lead.* Gotham Books.

Carlzon, J. (1987). *Moments of truth.* Ballinger Publishing Company.

Collins, J. (2001). *Good to great: Why some companies make the leap... and others don't.* Harper Business.

Collins, J., & Porras, J. I. (1994). *Built to last: Successful habits of visionary companies.* Harper Business.

Covey, S. R. (1989). *The 7 habits of highly effective people: Powerful lessons in personal change.* Free Press.

Dator, J. (2009). Alternative futures at the Manoa School. *Journal of Futures Studies, 14*(2), 1–18.

Dweck, C. S. (2006). *Mindset: The new psychology of success.* Random House.

Hagan, A. (n.d.). *Strategic foresight and leadership frameworks.*

Inayatullah, S. (2008). Six pillars: Futures thinking for transforming. *Foresight, 10*(1), 4–21.

Kim, W. C., & Mauborgne, R. (2005). *Blue ocean strategy: How to create uncontested market space and make the competition irrelevant.* Harvard Business Review Press.

McChesney, C., Covey, S., & Huling, J. (2012). *The 4 disciplines of execution: Achieving your wildly important goals.* Free Press.

Scharmer, O. (2009). *Theory U: Leading from the future as it emerges.* Berrett-Koehler.

Sharma, R. (2010). *The leader who had no title: A modern fable on real success in business and in life.* Simon & Schuster.

Thiel, P. (2014). *Zero to one: Notes on startups, or how to build the future.* Crown Business.

Wickman, G. (2011). *Traction: Get a grip on your business.* BenBella Books.

Willink, J., & Babin, L. (2015). *Extreme ownership: How U.S. Navy SEALs lead and win.* St. Martin's Press.

Wilson, M. (2023). *Shift: Everyday actions leaders can take to shift culture.* The People Game.